MY STORY

REGGIE: the L.A. Gator

DONUTS

PIZZA

Written and Illustrated by
ANGI MA WONG

ISBN 1-928753-12-4
ISBN-13: 978-1-928753-12-4
Written and illustrated by Angi Ma Wong
Pacific Heritage Books, Box 998, Palos Verdes Estates, CA 90274-0998 USA
For information/author contact/speaking:
Call 1-888-810-9891   E: angi@PacificHeritageBooks.com
www.PacificHeritageBooks.com
Printed in Hong Kong

Photo credits:
Fred Haney, p. 4
Desiree Wong, Pg. 2, pp. 9–11, 14–16
Efrain Iniguez, Back cover, pp.17–21
Tom Underhill/*Palos Verdes Peninsula News* © 2006, p.2
Sean Hiller/*Daily Breeze* © 2007, p.24.

A wife, mother of four, two-time cancer survivor and a lifelong educator, ANGI MA WONG is the best-selling and award-winning author of more than 25 titles. These include: Beatty award nominee *Night of the Red Moon,* best-selling *Reggie the L.A. Gator* (both for ages 8 and up) and the *Feng Shui Dos and Taboos* series, and *Who Ate My Socks* (ages 4–8). With a passion for family literacy, Wong shares her love for reading, writing, illustrating and publishing with audiences of all ages. Her next project *Beyond Compass, Paper and Gunpowder: China's Gifts to the World,* showcases Chinese inventions and discoveries that have changed the world.

My name is Reggie and I am an alligator. I live in Los Angeles, California. This is my own true story about how I became the most famous alligator in the world.

There are many people who love and own cats and dogs. They keep them as pets to play with and keep them company so they won't be lonely.

Other people keep fish, birds, mice, gerbils, skunks, pigs, snakes or rabbits for their pets.

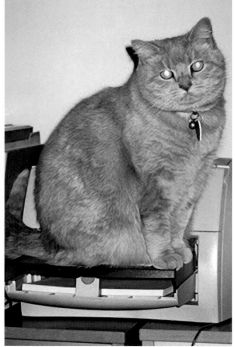

ut there are many animals that are poisonous, very big or strong. Sometimes they do or eat things naturally that make them dangerous. They cannot be kept at home because they might hurt the people around them. Among these animals are lions, tigers, bears and alligators.

When I was little, I lived in San Pedro, a part of the City of Los Angeles (L.A.), California, in the United States of America.

The man who owned me had four alligators, scorpions, piranha fish, and snapping turtles in his home. He fed us pet food, leftover pizza and jelly donuts.

During one spring, my owner decided that I was too big. It cost him too much money to feed me. He didn't want me for a pet any more. Instead of finding a new home for me, he thought of another way to get rid of me.

When we were growing up, he kept all the alligators in a plastic wading pool in his back yard. As we got bigger, we were moved to a very long, heated swimming pool.

I was an American alligator, a different kind than the others, so I ate much more food. As the years passed, I grew up to be a lot bigger too.

The place where he and a friend left me was in the big Machado Lake at the Ken Malloy Harbor Regional Park. It was in Harbor City, not far from San Pedro. The lake collected rain and other water from the City of Los Angeles.

Blue heron

Bullock's oriole

Egret

During that August, I discovered many of the 200 different kinds of birds in the park. These birds lived or rested there when they flew from Canada to South America before each winter and back again in the spring.

Ducks, sea gulls, geese, turtles, frogs and crayfish too, made their homes in the grass, marshes and trees around my new lake home.

Tree swallow

park ranger happened to see me in the middle of the lake one day. He told somebody who told somebody else who took my picture.

Within a few days, many people came down to the park to see me. They heard the news on the radio and saw me in newspapers, on the internet and television.

All summer long, there were helicopters in the sky and television and news vans lined up on the shore. In September, lots of people were laughing, singing and making music at the park. Some of them wore alligator costumes at this big party!

Maybe people came because they had never seen an alligator before. Maybe they wanted a close-up look at my glowing gold eyes that don't have eyelids. Maybe they wanted to catch me out of the water to find out if I really only had claws on the inside three toes of my two back feet. Maybe people wanted to see my big upper teeth that showed when my mouth was closed. Or maybe people were just curious because nobody knew how old I was or even if I was a boy or a girl alligator. (I'm a boy alligator.)

I liked playing hide and seek with all those people. I sometimes popped my head and nose out of the lake. At other times, I just hid in the tall grass or underwater where nobody could see me.

Can you find me?

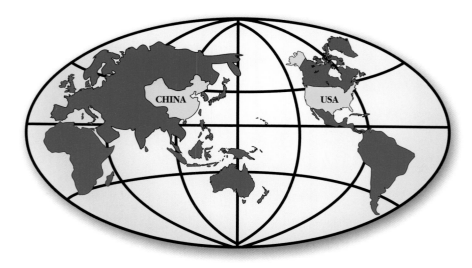

Everybody thought I was pretty special because alligators have been on the planet Earth for more than 200 million years. But we are only found in two countries in the whole world: China and the United States of America. We are not native to California or the west coast of the North American continent.

In my country, alligators are found in the states of Louisiana, Florida, Texas, Oklahoma, Arkansas, Mississippi, Alabama, Georgia, North Carolina, South Carolina and along the Gulf of Mexico.

My story and pictures were sent all over the world, even to faraway places like Singapore, Hong Kong and to Europe.

Songs and books were written about me. One book even had an alligator toy to go with it. The soft, fluffy animal looked just like me, wearing a REGGIE the L.A. Gator shirt.

See in yellow on the map where alligators are found in the U.S.A.

There were some City people who said that I might hurt the park's visitors. They put up signs and orange plastic fencing along the edge of the lake.

They wanted to catch and send me to live in a zoo. A zoo is a very large place where animals and birds live near each other. Many people can go there to see them and learn about the different kinds of living things found on Earth.

Visiting a zoo helps visitors understand more about animals such as where they come from, how they lived a long, long time ago, and now. People find out how to keep these wonderful living creatures and our planet safe, for today and always.

The City people called five different men to come to Los Angeles to catch me. They rode in boats or paddled kayaks in Machado Lake looking all over for me. They set traps using big pieces of chicken as bait to try and get me to come out of hiding.

But I wasn't interested because the lake already had lots of things that I could eat such as turtles, ducks, crayfish, snails and frogs.

When the weather became cooler in the autumn, I began to hibernate. It is a time when many animals such as bears and alligators, rest or sleep through the winter. When they wake up in the spring, they eat a lot of food because they are hungry.

I lived quietly in Lake Machado and didn't come out for many months. Nobody saw me except during July of my second summer. That's when I popped my head out of the water and surprised a lady who was taking pictures of birds.

nother year passed and my second winter
hibernation was over. It was now spring again
and both my head and tail had grown bigger. I was over
seven feet long now and stayed in a beautiful, hidden cove.
Every day I left the water to sun myself on the grassy bank.

One day I swam to the middle of Machado Lake and
slowly lifted my head to take a look around. A ranger
happened to look out at the water that April morning and
saw me. Soon the people and the news vans and the helicopters all came back to the park. Suddenly, I became a
radio, newspaper, internet and television star all over again.

Reggie's secret cove

In late May, I was taking a mid-afternoon nap on the south shore when two park rangers saw me. They called for help and some firefighters arrived first. Within minutes they were joined by over a dozen City, park and other people, all crowding into my cove!

Sneaking up behind my back, one of them covered my head with a dark cloth and looped a rope around it.

Meanwhile someone secretly watched my favorite cove and learned that I liked snoozing at that same sunny spot that was my home.

A huge wire fence with gates was built to go around the whole area where I came out of the lake to sunbathe.

I was surrounded as they all ganged up against me. Two men jumped on my back, grabbing and holding me down. But I put up a good fight, trying hard to scare all those people away by hissing and thrashing my tail.

hey used wide silver tape to keep my jaws shut because they thought I would bite. I was even blindfolded so I couldn't see.

Many arms bundled me up and put me into a yellow plastic sling. And just like that, I was carried away from my home in Lake Machado.

This is the last picture of me in my cove before I was captured.

PLEASE WASH
OUT THIS
KENNEL AREA IN
THIS VEHICLE
AFTER AN
ANIMAL HAS
BEEN PLACED IN
IT.

THANK YOU.

My tail hung out over the sling as the firefighters and park staff carried me to a special truck. It was used to pick up stray animals found on the streets and it had two doors. The truck's cage door clanged shut first and then another door was closed with a thump. I was locked inside to keep me safe on my trip.

The park police, with lights flashing on top of their cars, surrounded the big, white truck that would take me to the Los Angeles Zoo. News helicopters flew overhead while television vans and other cars followed. They made a long line behind us in a caravan as we left the park.

There are more famous people working and living in Los Angeles than in any place in the whole world. I was treated like one of these very famous or important people. My truck was leading a motorcade during the busiest traffic time.

We drove north on the Harbor Freeway and then the Pasadena Freeway, passing big hotels and bank buildings. We even went through four tunnels on the way to the zoo at Griffith Park.

Of course I was given the star treatment! After all, I used to be just an unwanted pet left in a park lake. Now I am Reggie the L.A. Gator, the most famous alligator in the world. Come and visit me at my new home at the Los Angeles Zoo.

*But if you tame me, then
we shall need each other.*

*To me, you will be unique
in all the world.*

*To you, I will be unique
in all the world . . .*

*You will become responsi-
ble forever for what you have
tamed . . .*

Antoine de Saint-Exupery
(1900–1944)
The Little Prince

EPILOGUE:

Six days after Reggie was moved into his new home at the zoo, the L.A. Gator escaped by climbing over a back fence.

Fortunately he did not go far and was returned safely.

Los Angeles Zoo information:
www.lazoo.org

CONSERVATION RESOURCES

www.greenigsociety.org The Green Iguana Society is dedicated to providing quality information on iguana care as well as information on current iguana adoptions and rescues throughout the United States and Canada.

www.corhs.org Colorado Reptile Humane Society works to improve the lives of reptiles and amphibians in captivity and in the wild through education and action.

www.baskingspot.com The Basking Spot is the internet spot for herpetelogical news and links.

www.anapsid.org Melissa Kaplans' Herp and Green Iguana Information collection.

www.crocodilian.com Crocodilians: Natural History and Conservation is the Internet's largest crocodile site, established in 1995. Written by a crocodile specialist, it's an ever-growing database of everything you need to know about crocodiles, including the different species, their biology, conservation, how they talk, and even their captive care.

www.ircf.org The International Reptile Conservation Foundation works to conserve reptiles and the natural habitats and ecosystems that support them.

www.michiganreptilerescue.org Mid-Michigan Reptile Rescue offers rescue, rehabilitation and adoption placement services for abandoned, abused and unwanted reptiles and exotics, as well providing educational opportunities for the general public.

www.herpcenter.com The Herp Center Network, more than just a website, is an online community. The HCN offers active forum discussion and educational resources all within the boundaries of a family-oriented website.